CLASSIC ROCK BANDS

THE BEATLES

by Judy Dodge Cummings

CONTENT CONSULTANT
Shaugn O'Donnell
Music Department Chair
The City College of New York

An Imprint of Abdo Publishing | abdobooks.com

abdobooks.com

Published by Abdo Publishing, a division of ABDO, PO Box 398166, Minneapolis, Minnesota 55439. Essential Library™ is a trademark and logo of Abdo Publishing.

Printed in the United States of America, North Mankato, Minnesota.
052021
092021

Cover Photo: Press Association/PA Wire URN: 44900853/AP Images
Interior Photos: AP Images, 4–5, 7, 38–39, 42, 45, 55; Gems/Redferns/Getty Images, 12–13; Keystone-France/Gamma-Keystone/Getty Images, 16, 18, 74–75; Michael Ochs Archives/Getty Images, 23, 53; Noyan Yalcin/Shutterstock Images, 24; Keystone/Hulton Archive/Getty Images, 26–27; Shutterstock Images, 28–29; Dean Mirrorpix/Newscom, 32; Press Association/PA Wire URN: 17170339/AP Images, 48–49; Peter Kemp/AP Images, 58–59; Bettmann/Getty Images, 62; Mirrorpix/Getty Images, 66–67; Cummings Archives/Redferns/Getty Images, 71; Daily Mirror/Mirrorpix/Getty Images, 80–81; Imma Gambardella/Shutterstock Images, 85; Tony Camerano/AP Images, 88–89; Pat Sullivan/AP Images, 92; Bob Grieser/AP Images, 94; Debby Wong/Shutterstock Images, 96

Editor: Melissa York
Series Designer: Colleen McLaren

Library of Congress Control Number: 2019953790

Publisher's Cataloging-in-Publication Data

Names: Dodge Cummings, Judy, author.
Title: The Beatles / by Judy Dodge Cummings
Description: Minneapolis, Minnesota : Abdo Publishing, 2022 | Series: Classic rock bands | Includes online resources and index.
Identifiers: ISBN 9781532191992 (lib. bdg.) | ISBN 9781532179891 (ebook)
Subjects: LCSH: Beatles--Juvenile literature. | Rock and roll bands--Biography--Juvenile literature. | Rock musicians--England--Biography--Juvenile literature. | Rock and roll music--Juvenile literature.
Classification: DDC 782.42166--dc23

CONTENTS

CHAPTER ONE

Ladies and Gentlemen, the Beatles!

On February 7, 1964, fans packed London's Heathrow Airport to give the Beatles a grand send-off. The band members—John Lennon, Paul McCartney, George Harrison, and Ringo Starr—were used to being treated like celebrities in Britain. Over the past year, "Beatlemania" had swept their homeland. Hysterical fans swarmed nightclubs when the band was performing, teenage girls wrote messages on the band's van in lipstick, and sales of their records soared. But this trip was different. The Beatles were going to the United States. No British pop star had ever conquered America. Prior to the Beatles' arrival, US journalists

The Beatles' arrival in New York in February 1964 would boost the band to new heights of fame.

N704PA
PAN AM
PAN AM
THE BEATLES
EUROPEAN AIRWAYS

reported less on their music and more on their long hairstyles, which some described as moptops with "sheep-dog bangs."[1]

The Beatles felt nervous. Although their song "I Want to Hold Your Hand" had reached the top of *Billboard* magazine's Hot 100 Singles chart, McCartney was pessimistic. The United States invented rock and roll. "What are we going to give them that they don't already have?" he wondered.[2]

As the plane landed at New York City's John F. Kennedy Airport, the terminal came into view. Faces pressed against the building's plate glass windows. People lined the building's roof and hung over its balconies. The crowd numbered at least 5,000.[3] "Who is this for?" McCartney asked.[4] The Beatles assumed someone important was flying in.

As the Beatles disembarked, they realized the crowd was for them. A line of 100 police struggled to hold back screaming fans. A girl on the terminal's third-floor balcony leaned out over the railing. Held aloft by companions, she screamed, "Here I am!"[5] A hydraulic crane used for lifting and lowering heavy machinery and parts was parked on the tarmac. When its driver began to move the crane, photographers hopped aboard and hung on, desperate for a good shot of the band.

Four chauffeur-driven Cadillacs pulled up to the terminal entrance. Two police officers carried

A mass of fans gathered to see the Beatles when they arrived at John F. Kennedy Airport.

each Beatle through the sea of fans to the band's waiting cars. A photographer grabbed a handful of McCartney's hair, testing whether the moptop was a wig. A cop told the chauffeur at the head of the line, "Get out of here, buddy, if you want to get out alive."[6] That evening the Beatles' arrival was the top news story, but not all coverage was positive.

The radio station WNEW reported that the Beatles' song "I Want to Hold Your Hand" made some people "want to hold their noses."[7]

The Beatles were scheduled to appear on the *Ed Sullivan Show* on February 9. The variety show had broadcast the rock and roll revolution as it happened. Elvis Presley had performed three times in the late 1950s, and in 1960, Smokey Robinson and the Supremes had been on the show. The program could open up the vast US market to the Beatles.

Teasing the Press

When faced with a rude question from a reporter, the Beatles typically responded with a witty comeback. When one journalist demanded to know why Harrison was not wearing a tie, he asked her, "Why aren't you wearing a hat?"[8] When another reporter asked Lennon, "Are you going to have a haircut while you're in America?," Lennon said, "We had one yesterday."[9] When Harrison was asked whether they had a leading lady in mind for a film they intended to make, he said, "We're trying to get the Queen. She sells."[10]

"ELVIS IS DEAD, LONG LIVE THE BEATLES"

At dawn on February 8, 13-year-old Irene Katz told her parents she was going to a friend's house to study. This was a lie. Katz and her friend went to New York City's Plaza Hotel, where the Beatles were staying. For nine hours, the girls waited on the sidewalk with dozens of fans, hoping the

Beatles would make an appearance. Katz brought a homemade sign that read, "Elvis Is Dead, Long Live the Beatles."[11] Elvis Presley represented yesterday's music to her. The Beatles were the new sound of the 1960s.

The next day on the *Ed Sullivan Show*, Lennon, McCartney, Harrison, and Starr performed for a television audience of 73 million, or 60 percent of all US television viewers.[12] These four British men with strange hairstyles, shiny black suits, and contagious smiles sang five songs. When the cameras cut to the audience, viewers at home saw teenage girls screaming and weeping in ecstasy.

The press was not kind. The following day, the *New York Herald* described the Beatles as "75 per cent publicity, 20 per cent haircut and 5 per cent lilting lament."[13] The *Washington Post* called the band members "homely."[14] *Newsweek* said, "Visually they are a nightmare. . . . Musically they are a near disaster."[15]

"I have never seen any scenes to compare with the bedlam that was occasioned by their debut. Broadway was jammed with people for almost eight blocks. They screamed, yelled, and stopped traffic."[16]

– Ed Sullivan, describing the Beatles' first appearance on his show on February 9, 1964

A Lucky Layover

It was chance that brought the Beatles to the attention of television host Ed Sullivan. On October 31, 1963, Sullivan was passing through the London airport at the same time the Beatles were returning from a tour. Hundreds of screaming fans packed the airport terminal, and Sullivan asked a staff member what was going on. "The Beatles," the staffer replied. "Who the hell are the Beatles?" Sullivan wondered.[18] Two weeks later, he was negotiating with Beatles manager Brian Epstein to bring the band on his show.

Young fans like Irene Katz were better predictors of the future than the music critics were. The band appeared on the music scene at a pivotal moment. After World War II (1939–1945), there was a baby boom, and by 1964 these babies were teenagers. The early 1960s were a time of unprecedented prosperity in the West, so these young people had money to spend. Millions of teens chose to spend their money on the upbeat music of the Beatles—songs that felt like a soundtrack for their generation. By the end of 1964, the Beatles had 28 songs on *Billboard*'s Hot 100 Singles chart, including 11 that had made the Top 10.[17]

The Beatles helped create the counterculture movement of the 1960s. Unafraid to experiment, the Beatles continually evolved their sound and style, setting new standards for rock and roll. From their working-class roots in Liverpool, England, the Beatles rose to become the best-selling rock band in history.

"Now what happened with the Beatles was that they were the first real group where there was no one single individual who was the center of attention. . . . Suddenly you had a four-piece band that played their own instruments . . . and America was ready for them."[19]

– Cliff Richards, British pop star

CHAPTER TWO

The Beginning

Sixteen-year-old John Lennon was blown away the first time he heard Elvis Presley sing "Heartbreak Hotel" on the radio in 1956. The teenager from Liverpool, England, could hardly understand a word Elvis said, but that did not matter. The sound moved him. In an interview years later, Lennon described the song's impact on him: "My whole life changed from then on. I was just completely shaken by it."[1] In the late 1950s, radio stations played light orchestra music and singers who crooned like Frank Sinatra. Elvis's bluesy lament with its bold beat skyrocketed to the top of American and British music charts.

Lennon grew up in Liverpool, England, where he listened to rock music as an adolescent.

But Lennon and countless other British teens did not just want to listen to rock music. They wanted to play it. British musician Lonnie Donegan was a trailblazer who modeled a musical style many British teens, including Lennon, would follow. In 1954, Donegan, a British banjo player, recorded the American folk song "Rock Island Line" in skiffle style. Skiffle, originally from the American South, was music played on homemade instruments. Inspired by Donegan's version of "Rock Island Line," aspiring British musicians got busy. Broom handles tied to wooden boxes and strung with wire became bass guitars. Tin trash can lids and washboards became drums. The skiffle craze swept the country.

THE BEATLES MEET

Since age five, Lennon had lived with his Aunt Mimi and Uncle George in Woolton, a suburb of Liverpool. Lennon's mother, Julia, lived nearby, but after her husband abandoned her when Lennon was a baby, she had struggled financially and emotionally. Julia's childless older sister Mimi offered to take in the boy. While Lennon still saw his mother regularly, Aunt Mimi was his caretaker and disciplinarian. As such, she was the person he begged to buy him a guitar when he was 16. Mimi finally gave in and bought Lennon a guitar, after which he was rarely seen without it. "The guitar's all very well, John," Mimi told her nephew, "but you'll never make a living at it."[2] Lennon kept strumming.

In 1956, Lennon and some friends from Quarry Bank High School formed a skiffle band called the Quarrymen. They played at school dances and local churches. On July 6, 1957, while playing at a festival in Woolton, Lennon met another guitar player—Paul McCartney.

McCartney, also from Liverpool, was two years younger than Lennon. After his mother died of breast cancer when he was 14, McCartney found solace in music. His father had been an amateur musician, and he purchased a guitar for McCartney. Michael McCartney, Paul's brother, told Hunter Davis, the author of the biography *The Beatles*, "The minute he got the guitar, that was the end. . . . He played in the lavatory, in the bath, everywhere."[4]

Loss of a Mother

Although Lennon lived with his aunt and uncle while he was growing up, his mother, Julia, still played an important part in his life, especially when Lennon reached his teenage years. Unlike Aunt Mimi, Julia put few restrictions on him. When Lennon was 17, his mother was killed by a car as she was crossing the street. "It was the worst thing that ever happened to me," Lennon said. "We could communicate. We got on. She was great."[3] He memorialized his mother in the 1968 song "Julia."

Paul McCartney, *front*, with his older brother Michael in 1948

On that fateful July evening, McCartney watched the Quarrymen play. "John played the lead guitar," he recalled. "But he played it like a banjo."[5] Lennon's mother played banjo, and all he knew were the few chords she had taught him.

After the festival, McCartney performed for the Quarrymen to demonstrate his skills. Lennon was impressed because McCartney could tune a guitar and because he knew so many song lyrics. At that moment, Lennon had a decision to make. He could forget about McCartney and keep his position as the best performer in the Quarrymen, or he could make the band stronger by asking McCartney to join. Lennon invited him into the group.

Almost immediately, McCartney did two things that shaped the future of the Beatles. First, he showed Lennon some songs he had written himself. Inspired, Lennon began to compose his own music. McCartney also suggested they invite a guitar-playing friend of his, George Harrison, to join the band.

Harrison grew up the youngest of four children in a working-class family in a suburb of Liverpool. A bright but reluctant student, Harrison attended the Liverpool Institute, the same school as McCartney. Like many British boys, in his early teens Harrison was swept up by the music of Lonnie Donegan. But instead of a homemade guitar, his mother

Harrison was an avid guitar player from a young age.

bought him a quality electric one, and Harrison taught himself to play. Harrison was younger than McCartney, but they rode the same bus and developed a friendship from a shared passion for guitars.

Sometime in 1957, McCartney invited Harrison to hear the Quarrymen play at a local club. McCartney introduced Harrison to Lennon, and Harrison played a few songs on his guitar. Lennon was impressed that the 14-year-old Harrison knew more chords than anyone else in the band, but he thought Harrison was too young to be a Quarryman.

For months, Harrison followed the band around from one gig to another, with his guitar in tow. Sometimes Harrison

Schoolboys

Lennon, McCartney, and Harrison all grew up in Liverpool. As a teenager, Lennon enjoyed pulling pranks and getting into fights. His favorite part of school was study hall, when he filled notebooks with cartoons, poetry, and funny stories.

In contrast, McCartney did well in school. He was accepted to the Liverpool Institute, the best secondary school in Liverpool. But when he reached his teens, McCartney said, "All I wanted was women, money, and clothes."[6]

Harrison rebelled against school rules through his appearance. He wore his hair long and used his mother's sewing machine to stitch an extra seam in his trousers, making them skintight. Sometimes Harrison wore a canary-yellow vest under his school uniform blazer. The teachers hated it, but Harrison was proud, later bragging, "I always managed to keep a bit of individuality."[7]

filled in for absent band members. In 1958, without an official invitation, the 15-year-old Harrison simply became a Quarryman.

Other band members came and went, but Lennon, McCartney, and Harrison stayed. The group abandoned skiffle and focused on rock and roll. But they knew any decent rock band needed two things: a drummer and a good name.

BECOMING THE BEATLES

By 1959, Lennon had graduated, and because neither McCartney nor Harrison was connected to the Quarry school, the band decided to choose a new name. For a while they became Johnny and the Moondogs. Then Lennon enrolled at art school, where he met another student, Cynthia Powell, and they began dating. Lennon also befriended fellow student Stuart Sutcliffe, and Sutcliffe joined the band as a bass guitarist. Because the group played many college dances, they became the College Band.

In the spring of 1960, the band was hired to accompany singer Johnny Gentle on a two-week tour of Scotland. For this event they wanted a name people could remember, like the famous American rock band the Crickets had. Someone suggested they pick a different insect, so the band became the

Silver Beetles. By August 1960, they were known simply as the Beatles.

GERMANY AND A DRUMMER

In the late summer of 1960, Liverpool nightclub owner Allan Williams contacted the Beatles. A businessman he knew in Hamburg, Germany, was looking for a rock group for a long-term gig at his nightclub. Williams told the Beatles the job was theirs if they could find a drummer.

The Beatles knew someone who might fit the bill. The band had played a few shows at the Casbah, a new club in Liverpool. It was owned by Mona Best, and her son Pete Best was a drummer. Pete's band had recently broken up, so McCartney asked him to join the Beatles and come to Hamburg. Pete agreed.

Hamburg was a working-class seaport similar to Liverpool. Initially, the Beatles

Teddy Boys

Before the Beatles left for Germany in 1960, they dressed in what was called the teddy boy style when they performed. This was a fashion craze for young British men in the late 1950s. Teddy boys wore velvet-tipped jackets, frilled shirts, and narrow pants. They greased their hair, sweeping the sides past the ears to form two flaps like the wings of a duck. The Beatles also added a western flair with black-and-white cowboy shirts and neckties made from black shoelaces.

While playing with Rory Storm and the Hurricanes, Starkey had a pompadour hairstyle.

played at a club called the Indra, living in a dirty storeroom at a nearby theater. It wasn't glamorous, but for the first time the Beatles had a steady job playing rock music.

Eventually, the Beatles moved to the Kaiserkeller, a club where another Liverpool band, Rory Storm and the Hurricanes, also worked. The bands alternated hours on stage. The drummer for the Hurricanes was Richard Starkey, and he sat in with the Beatles a couple of times. Starkey's stage name was Ringo Starr.

> "In Hamburg we got very good as a band because we had to play eight hours a night and we started building a big repertoire of some of our own songs, but mainly we did all the old rock songs. . . . We got very tight as a band."[9]
>
> *– George Harrison*

Hamburg honed the Beatles' skills. In Liverpool their sets only lasted an hour. In Hamburg, the band played for six to eight hours. The Beatles needed to learn new songs and new entertainment strategies. The fact that their audience was German made them work harder. "We had to . . . put our heart and soul into it," McCartney said, to communicate the music's meaning.[8] The Germans loved it when the Beatles played at

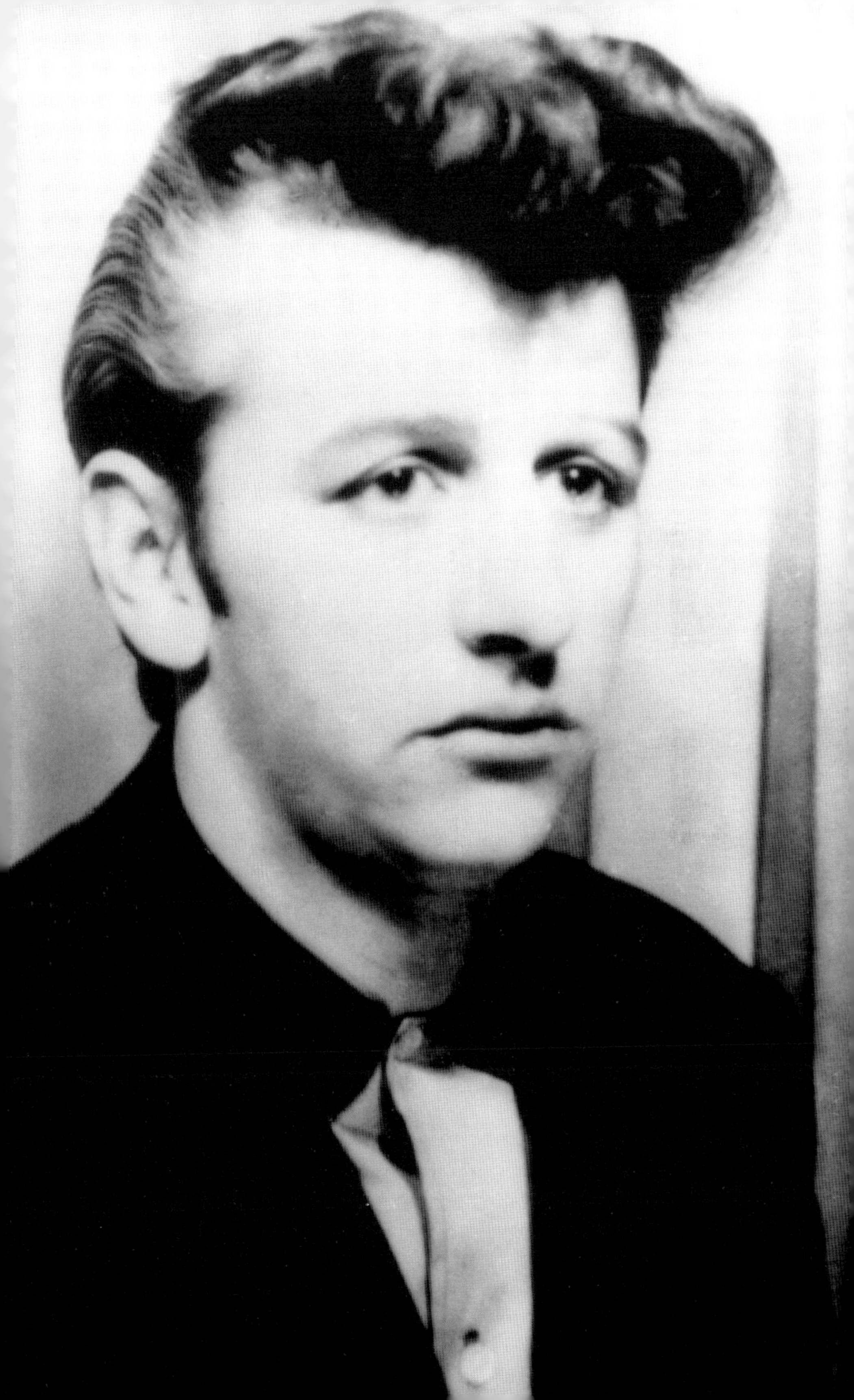

Stylized statues in Hamburg represent the time the Beatles spent in the city in 1960.

an earsplitting level, so high volume became part of the band's style.

Hamburg also transformed the Beatles' style. The men arrived in Germany wearing sports coats and pressed trousers. Soon they were dressed in black leather jackets, T-shirts, and blue jeans. The Beatles even purchased cowboy boots and tailored leather pants.

In November 1960, McCartney and Pete Best were deported from Germany after being accused of arson for lighting a small fire to see in the dark in the movie theater where they were staying. In December, the German government discovered that Harrison was underage for a legal work permit, and he was ordered to leave the country. At the same time, for unknown reasons, Lennon's work permit was also revoked. Feeling dispirited, the Beatles returned to Britain, uncertain of their future.

CHAPTER THREE

British Beatlemania

While the Beatles were in Hamburg, the British rock scene changed. Musical groups began imitating each other. Everyone wore gray suits and polished shoes and danced in tight choreographed formation. Their music was as restrained as their appearance. In contrast, the Beatles looked scruffy and disorganized, and their music was loud and wild.

The impact of the band on British teens was evident at a Beatles concert on December 27, 1960, at the Litherland Town Hall. The young people loved the Beatles' raucous music, and the more excited the crowd became, the freer the band felt.

In 1960, Harrison, Lennon, and McCartney were still a few years away from international stardom.

The Cavern Club closed in the 1970s, but it later reopened in its original location.

"It was that evening," said Lennon, "that we really came out of our shell and let go as we'd played in Hamburg."[1] The teenagers went crazy, with girls screaming and boys fighting.

LOCAL FAME

By early 1961, the Beatles were regulars at the Cavern Club, a well-known spot in Liverpool's

center. Word spread, and the Beatles gained a solid fan base. Then in April, the Beatles headed back to Hamburg to play 92 nights at the Top Ten Club. Sutcliffe left the band to study art, so McCartney became the bass guitar player. Although the Beatles were glad to have regular work, they were also frustrated. They seemed destined to be stuck between Liverpool and Hamburg. Then the Beatles got a bit of luck.

A German producer asked the band to perform backup for singer Tony Sheridan on a single. The song, "My Bonnie," was a traditional tune. Normally played in a slow and steady rhythm, it was a plaintive love song. The Beatles played the song faster and louder than anyone had heard it played before, with their electric guitars and drums turning a folk song into rock and roll. The record sold well in Germany and was played frequently on Radio Luxembourg, a station that could be heard in England.

> "In those old Cavern days half the thing was just ad lib; what you'd call comedy. We just used to mess about, jump into the audience, do anything."[2]
>
> *– John Lennon*

After returning to Liverpool in the summer of 1961, the Beatles played a lot of gigs. However, they still lived with their families because the band members could not support themselves off their music. They began feeling pressure to get "real jobs." Then the Beatles met someone who turned their small-scale success into a global phenomenon.

ENTER BRIAN EPSTEIN

Down the block from the Cavern Club was the North End Music Store (NEMS), the most famous record store in Liverpool. Twenty-seven-year-old Brian Epstein managed this family-owned business. Epstein's goal was to stock every record ever made. If customers could not find what they wanted in NEMS, Epstein vowed to find the record and deliver it.

On October 28, 1961, a customer entered NEMS and asked Epstein for a record called "My Bonnie," featuring the Beatles. Epstein did not have the record and had never heard of the Beatles, but he vowed to locate it. Over the next couple days, he phoned other record dealers. They had not heard of the Beatles either. A few days later, two girls came in also looking for "My Bonnie." They told Epstein the Beatles played at the Cavern. He went to the club to check them out.

Epstein's first impression of the Beatles was mixed. "They were not very tidy and not very clean," he said.[3] They smoked and ate and chatted while they performed. But, he explained, "They seemed to give off some sort of personal magnetism. I was fascinated by them."[4]

Epstein came to the Cavern again and again. As he watched the Beatles, an attempt to sell their records evolved into a dream of managing

Epstein played a key role in shaping the band's early career.

the band. On December 3, 1961, he invited the Beatles to his office to talk business. Two weeks later, the Beatles signed a contract making Epstein their manager.

Epstein professionalized the Beatles. From then on, they wrote down set lists, or lists of the songs they were going to play and their order. They stopped eating and drinking during performances. The Beatles had to wear suits, not street clothes. Epstein also negotiated better pay from the owners of the clubs where the Beatles played and got them another stint in Hamburg.

PETE BEST IS OUT

Week after week, Epstein carted recordings of the Beatles' songs from record company to record company, trying to find someone willing to sign a contract with the band. He had no luck. Tired of hauling the recordings around, Epstein went to a store in London to have all the songs put on one record. The store was part of EMI, a huge music company that had been in business since the 1930s.

The technician who helped Epstein liked the Beatles' sound. He told his superiors, and word of the Beatles reached the ear of George Martin. He was a record producer with Parlophone Records, an imprint of EMI. After listening to the Beatles' record, Martin wanted to audition them. "Congratulations boys," Epstein wrote in a telegram to the Beatles, who were in Hamburg at the time. "EMI request recording session. Please rehearse new material."[5] The band auditioned for Martin in June 1962. They played four songs that Lennon and McCartney had written, including "Love Me Do" and "P.S. I Love You."

A few weeks later, Martin told Epstein that he wanted the Beatles to sign a contract with Parlophone. Lennon, McCartney, and Harrison were thrilled, but they did not tell Best. Instead, Epstein called Best into his office. "The boys want you out," Epstein told him, "and Ringo in."[6] The news hit Best like a punch in the stomach. Epstein said Martin did not like Best's drumming, and the other Beatles did not think he was a good fit. When the news hit the streets,

Ringo Starr

Richard Starkey was born on July 7, 1940, in one of the poorest neighborhoods of Liverpool. Serious illnesses caused Starkey to miss a lot of school, and he withdrew completely at age 15. During England's skiffle craze, his stepfather bought him a drum set, and Starkey formed a band. Eventually, he became the drummer for Rory Storm and the Hurricanes, Liverpool's leading rock band at the time. Also at this time, Starkey adopted the stage name Ringo Starr. Starr was apprehensive about becoming a Beatle. He knew female fans loved Best because he was handsome. "Me, I was just a skinny, bearded scruff," Starr said. "Why get a bad-looking cat when you can get a good-looking one?"[7] But before long, fans adored Starr too.

there was pandemonium in Liverpool. Fans of Best picketed the Cavern, shouting "Pete Forever, Ringo Never."[8]

The Beatles had gotten to know Ringo Starr in Hamburg. The band Starr was with, Rory Storm and the Hurricanes, played at the same club as the Beatles. Starr had even played drums for the Beatles a few times when Best was sick. The Hurricanes were very popular in Britain, but when the Beatles asked Starr to join their band, they offered five pounds more per week than the Hurricanes. Starr said yes.

George Martin

Harrison said record producer George Martin was "always there for us to interpret our strangeness."[9] Martin's impact on the Beatles was evident from the beginning. In September 1962, when the Beatles were recording their second single, "Please Please Me," Martin thought the song sounded dreary. He told them to play it twice as fast. With this change, the song went to Number 1. Martin rearranged chords, suggested song titles, experimented with technology, and turned the Beatles' random whistles and hums into musical notes. Martin shaped the songs that became Beatles classics.

BREAKING OUT

The Parlophone Records Studio was located on Abbey Road in London. On September 11, 1962, the Beatles arrived to make a record they hoped would be their big break. At this time in history, vinyl records came in three sizes. The LP, or long-playing record, contained 20 minutes of music on each side. The EP, or extended play, held 7.5 minutes of music per side. The 45, named for the speed at which it was played in revolutions per minute, had just one song per side. That day the Beatles made a 45 with "Love Me Do" featured on the A side and "P.S. I Love You" on the B side.

After the 45 released on October 4, 1962, it crept up the music charts. Martin told the Beatles to keep making records. In January 1963, they released "Please, Please Me." In April the band put out its first LP, also titled *Please Please Me,* and its third single, "From Me to You." Epstein hired a band promoter who booked the Beatles for photo shoots, interviews, and tours. John, Paul, George, and Ringo had their names and faces splashed all over Britain. By September, the Beatles ruled the British record charts. *Please Please Me* was the top-selling LP, *Twist and Shout* was the top-selling EP, and "She Loves You" was the top-selling single.

On October 13, 1963, the Beatles performed at the London Palladium Theater, and it was this night when the British press finally recognized Beatlemania. However, it was not the Beatles' music the journalists reported on but their fans.

A crowd swarmed around the Palladium on the day of the concert. The post office delivered mountains of presents to the Beatles all day. Fans blocked the entrance to the stage door, and the four Beatles were almost mobbed as they dashed into the building. Fans outside the hall screamed so loudly the band could not rehearse. This intense, almost hysterical devotion was dubbed Beatlemania. It was clear that the Beatles had conquered Britain. Now they looked to the United States.

Mass Hysteria

The Beatles' fans exhibited devotion unlike anything the world had ever seen. Teenage girls screamed, fainted, and sobbed. Experts have tried to explain this mass hysteria. Writer Barbara Ehrenreich wrote that teen girls, expected to be prim and proper in the early 1960s, rebelled during Beatles concerts because there was safety in large groups. Psychologist Ruth Deller said fans valued the group identity they got from worshipping the Beatles. It was like belonging to a special club. Fan Jan Myers cannot explain the reasons for her love of the Beatles, but she admits, "I was just obsessed."[10]

CHAPTER FOUR

US Invasion

Although the Beatles were celebrities in Britain, American record labels were not interested in their songs. In early 1963, Epstein approached one recording company after another. No one was interested. Executives at American Capitol Records said, "We don't think the Beatles will do anything in this market."[1]

Unwilling to give up on an American record deal, Epstein returned to New York in November 1963. He knocked on the doors of Capitol Records again with a new song—"I Want to Hold Your Hand." The Beatles thought the song had "a sort of American spiritual sound."[2] Capitol Records

The year 1963 marked the beginning of the Beatles' rise to fame in the United States.

agreed to release the single, but not until January of 1964, and executives told Epstein they were not optimistic about the Beatles' prospects for success in the United States.

THE AMERICAN MOOD

The Beatles had not even arrived in the United States when the press began criticizing them. On November 22, a commentator on *CBS Morning News* said the Beatles were "non-hero[es] as they make non-music, wear non-haircuts. . ."[3] But no one paid attention to that commentary for long, because later that same day, tragedy struck the nation.

While riding in a motorcade in Dallas, Texas, President John F. Kennedy was assassinated. Kennedy had been only 43 when he was elected in 1960. For many, he symbolized a better future for the United States. Young people felt their hopes and dreams had been killed with their president. Then something came along to rekindle their excitement.

"I Want to Hold Your Hand"

"I Want to Hold Your Hand" revolutionized pop music. The song's rhythm was unorthodox and free spirited compared to those of other popular songs of the time. Lennon said that he and McCartney wrote the song "one on one, eyeball to eyeball" while sitting side by side at a piano.[4]

On December 10, a 15-year-old girl from Maryland watched a rebroadcast of the *CBS Morning News* program that aired the day Kennedy was shot. Curious about the Beatles, the girl wrote to her local radio station. The disc jockey did not have any Beatles music, so he contacted a flight attendant on a British airline. That attendant brought a copy of "I Want to Hold Your Hand" back to the United States and gave it to the radio station.

On the evening of December 17, 1963, the disc jockey played the single. It was the first time the song had been heard in the United States. Phone lines lit up. Listeners requested the song again and again, and stations across the nation played it.

Capitol Records realized they had a hit and sped up production of the record. "I Want to Hold Your Hand" was released in late December 1963, three weeks earlier than planned. By February 1, 1964, the single was Number 1 on the *Billboard* charts.

FIRST TASTE OF THE UNITED STATES

Frenzied fans followed the Beatles throughout their short visit to the United States. After the band's first performance on the *Ed Sullivan Show* on February 9, the Beatles traveled to Washington, DC, by train on February 11 to perform a concert. More than 3,000 teenagers flung themselves against

The Beatles played their first-ever US concert at the Coliseum, a venue in Washington, DC.

the tall platform gates at the city's Union Station when the Beatles arrived. While the band members performed at the Washington Coliseum, fans pelted them with buttons and hair curlers.

After that concert, the Beatles attended a charity ball at the British embassy. The men hated rubbing elbows with the elite and powerful. Starr said these people treated the Beatles like "something in a zoo," with one woman even snipping off a lock of his hair.[5]

After meeting the new president, Lyndon Johnson, and performing at Carnegie Hall in New York City, the Beatles flew to Miami, Florida, to tape their second live performance for the *Ed Sullivan Show*. Seven thousand fans met them at the airport, smashing dozens of windows and glass doors in the terminal. The band was housed in the luxurious Deauville Hotel, but it felt like a prison. The four dared not leave the hotel because of the mob of fans waiting outside.

Moptop Origins

On the Beatles' first trip to Hamburg, Stuart Sutcliffe became the boyfriend of a German woman, Astrid Kirchherr. She did not like Sutcliffe's teddy boy pompadour, so he allowed her to brush his hair forward. That night, when Sutcliffe showed up at the club, the other Beatles collapsed with laughter. Embarrassed, Sutcliffe brushed his hair back into his usual style. Kirchherr convinced him to give the new look another try. The band made fun of Sutcliffe again, but this time he stuck with Kirchherr's style. The next night, Harrison arrived at the club with his hair brushed forward too. Then McCartney and finally Lennon followed suit. That was how the Beatles' famous moptops began.

By April 4, less than two months after their *Ed Sullivan Show* appearances, the Beatles had 12 songs listed on the *Billboard* Hot 100 chart, including five songs that topped the list. The Beatles had successfully invaded the United States.

WHY DID THE UNITED STATES LOVE THE BEATLES?

Timing was one reason the Beatles succeeded in the United States when British rock performers before them failed. By the early 1960s, American rock and roll was disappearing. Elvis Presley, the biggest rock star of the 1950s, was drafted into the US Army. Young star Buddy Holly had died in a plane crash, and record companies and radio stations refused to play the music of Jerry Lee Lewis and Chuck Berry because both men had been accused of sexual misconduct.

With these stars silenced, American rock was stagnant. People were listening to soft pop. When the Beatles arrived on the scene, many of their songs were covers of rock songs that had been popular in the United States a decade earlier. The Beatles just freshened up most of these songs, but with a few, they remade the song's sound. One example of this is "Twist and Shout." That song had been recorded by the Isley Brothers, an American group. The Isley Brothers' rendition used sax and trumpets, and it did well on both pop charts and R&B charts. The Beatles turned it into an energetic party song. Starr hammered the drums and Lennon shrieked "C'mon, c'mon, c'mon baby now."[6] Fans loved it.

The band's onstage energy captured the imagination of fans around the world.

American rock shaped the Beatles' early music. They grew up listening to the Everly Brothers, Buddy Holly, the Shirelles, Chuck Berry, and Elvis. The Beatles put their own spin on these artists, but at its core, the band's early music was very much an American sound. In a way, the Beatles returned rock and roll to the United States.

The Beatles on Segregation

The Beatles were heavily influenced by African American musicians such as Marvin Gaye, the Miracles, Chuck Jackson, and Mary Wells. When the band members returned to the United States for a second tour in September 1964, they learned the concert hall in Jacksonville, Florida, was racially segregated, with the worst seats given to African Americans. The Beatles refused to accept this. The band sent out a press release stating, "We will not appear unless Negroes are allowed to sit anywhere."[9] City officials caved. The stadium was integrated, and the Beatles performed. After this, the Beatles added a clause to their contracts stating they would never perform to a segregated audience.

The Beatles also arrived at a time when the nation needed a distraction. After the assassination of President Kennedy, the country was sad and confused. Will Lee, a professional musician and member of Fab Faux, a Beatles tribute band, was 11 years old when Kennedy died. He said, "It was such a life-altering thing for this country. . . . It hit us so hard. . . . We kept looking for answers."[7]

Along came the Beatles. According to Lee, "There was a lot of fear and uncertainty in the air and the Beatles were this total distraction from that. They had all this positivity and it was something completely out of the realm of what we'd seen before."[8]

Once they had taken the United States by storm, the Beatles returned to Britain. It was time to begin the next phase of their careers—making movies and touring the world.

"They were doing things nobody was doing. Their chords were outrageous, just outrageous, and their harmonies made it all valid. . . . I knew they were pointing the direction of where music had to go."[10]

– Singer-songwriter Bob Dylan on the Beatles

CHAPTER FIVE

Making Movies and Touring the World

For the next two years, the Beatles maintained a brutal schedule. Each year, the band went on three long tours and produced one movie, three singles, and an album. Although they became increasingly skilled musicians, the four were tired of life on the road, and cracks began to appear in their relationships.

A HARD DAY'S NIGHT AND *HELP!*

In 1964, the Beatles signed a three-movie contract with United Artists. The band had fun making its first movie, *A Hard Day's Night*, but its second film, *Help!*, was an

Lennon, Starr, and McCartney during filming for *A Hard Day's Night*

TELEPHONES

experience the band members vowed never to repeat.

A Hard Day's Night was a fictional documentary of the Beatles' experiences as their fame skyrocketed. The madcap musical covered 36 hours in the life of the band as the Beatles traveled to London for a performance while dodging their fanatical fans. Lennon, McCartney, Harrison, and Starr played themselves. *A Hard Day's Night* premiered in London on July 6, 1964. The movie only cost $500,000 to make and earned $5.8 million at the box office, close to the equivalent of $50 million in 2020.

Help! was a different experience. While *A Hard Day's Night* was shot in England, *Help!* was filmed in Austria and the Bahamas. The Beatles had to follow a

Speedy Songwriters

The speed with which McCartney and Lennon wrote songs was part of their brilliance. While the Beatles were filming *A Hard Day's Night*, the pair also had to write the songs for the movie's soundtrack album. After weeks of work, the album lacked only the title track. At ten o'clock one night, producer Walter Shenson reminded McCartney and Lennon they needed to write that song, figuring they would get him a rough draft in a few days. However, the next morning McCartney handed Shenson matchbook covers with the lyrics of "A Hard Day's Night" scribbled on them. Then he and Lennon picked up their guitars and played the song. "A Hard Day's Night" went on to become a Number 1 hit.

script and act out roles. The plot centered on Starr. An admirer sent him a sacred ring from the Far East, and a religious fanatic was determined to kill Starr in order to get the ring back.

The Beatles did not enjoy making *Help!* Their costar, Victor Spinetti, blamed the script. He called the movie "a straitjacket of a film for the Beatles" because they did not enjoy acting.[1] The Beatles smoked marijuana regularly during the filming, a habit that did not help their motivation or memory when the cameras rolled. When *Help!* hit the theaters in August 1965, critics were lukewarm. It would be two years before the Beatles made another film.

EVOLVING MUSICAL STYLE

During 1965 and 1966, the Beatles churned out three albums at breakneck speed. *Help!*, released in August 1965, was largely a pop album. But the next two albums showed how the Beatles' sound was evolving.

Rubber Soul, released on December 3, 1965, was a transitional album—it was no longer pop, but it was not quite experimental rock. Harrison had picked up a sitar on the movie set for *Help!* and learned to play this Indian instrument. The sitar is featured for the first time on *Rubber Soul*, on the track "Norwegian Wood."

The Order of the British Empire

On June 12, 1965, the Queen of England announced that the Beatles had been made Members of the Order of the British Empire (MBE). This honor is given to people who make contributions in the arts and sciences or do charitable works. Some past recipients of the award objected, arguing that Queen Elizabeth had cheapened the award by giving it to a rock and roll band. One colonel even returned the 12 medals he had earned in World War I (1914–1918) and World War II (1939–1945) as an act of protest. Four years later, Lennon returned his own MBE to protest the British government's position on the Vietnam War (1954–1975). But he also joked that he was returning the award because he was upset that his single "Cold Turkey" had slipped in the charts.

The Beatles became involved in the technical end of the recording process, something the engineers and Martin had previously handled. The new technology of four-track recording allowed the band to produce more layered sounds. Instead of all four Beatles having to play simultaneously, the engineers could record vocals, rhythm, and instrumentals on different tracks and then overlay them into one final recording.

During recording for *Rubber Soul*, personality clashes began to appear. Engineer Norman Smith said, "Paul wanted to go one way and John wasn't maybe too keen. There was a certain turbulence. . . . Things didn't seem eye-to-eye between John and Paul."[2] Harrison and Starr

The iconic album cover for *Revolver* was designed by artist Klaus Voormann.

stayed away from these conflicts. Starr played cards until he had to play drums, and Harrison began composing his own songs.

Revolver, released on August 5, 1966, represented the beginning of the Beatles' experimental phase. The Beatles were using the hallucinogenic drug LSD by this time, and their drug use is reflected in both lyrics and sound. Lennon had read *The Psychedelic Experience*, a book about psychedelic drugs and the Buddhist religion. The book inspired him to write "Tomorrow Never Knows," a song about what LSD did to his psyche.

For this track, engineer Geoff Emerick used a special speaker, known as a Leslie speaker, to create a swirling sound. Harrison played an Indian stringed instrument called a tamboura. McCartney made tapes that imitated German experimental classical music, creating a sound like a guitar being tuned with a shrieking noise. Martin ran McCartney's tapes forward and backward through interconnected recorders, creating a unique, otherworldly effect. This collage of sound played as Lennon sang "Listen to the color of your dreams. It is not living, it is not living."[3] Indian instruments, technological innovations, and Lennon's dabbling in Buddhism gave *Revolver* a flavor unlike any music the Beatles had created so far.

FINAL TOUR

The Beatles typically took three long tours a year, one in Britain, one in the United States, and a third in Europe or Asia. Challenges on the road in 1966 convinced the band to give up touring.

Some in Japan protested the Beatles' trip to the country.

The Beatles received death threats when they played in Tokyo, Japan, from June 30 to July 2, 1966. Japanese nationalists were upset that the Beatles were playing at a martial arts hall, believing the band's presence desecrated the sacred space.

During the Beatles' concerts, police officers lined every aisle.

When the Beatles toured the United States from August 12 to August 29, 1966, they didn't experience physical threats, but they were beat up emotionally. Back in March, Lennon had given an interview in which he said, "We [the Beatles] are more popular than Jesus right now."[4] No one paid attention to Lennon's comments at the time. However, before the band arrived in August, the old interview was republished, and controversy erupted. A radio station in Birmingham, Alabama, held a bonfire where crowds burned Beatles albums and souvenirs. Twenty-two stations in the American South banned Beatles music from their airwaves.

The Price of Celebrity

It was not easy being the wife or girlfriend of a Beatle. After Harrison began to date actress Pattie Boyd, she received threatening letters from women who insisted they were his real girlfriends. One weekend, Harrison and Boyd, along with John and Cynthia Lennon, flew to Ireland for a private weekend. But they found no privacy. Hotel staff tapped the phones in the Beatles' rooms, and photographers and journalists followed the couples everywhere. To escape, the two women were smuggled out of the hotel in laundry baskets and driven to the airport in a laundry van.

The Beatles had had enough. The final concert of the US tour was on August 29, 1966, at Candlestick Park in San Francisco, California. The Beatles decided this would be their last live concert ever. This marked the end of the first stage of the Beatles' career. But much more was yet to come.

> "We'd had enough of performing forever. I couldn't imagine any reason that would have made us do any sort of tour again. We were all really tired."[5]
>
> *– John Lennon*

CHAPTER SIX

Experimentation

When the Beatles returned from their final tour in August 1966, they were ready for a long-awaited rest. A reporter asked what the end of touring meant for the band's future. Lennon said, "We cannot go on holding hands forever. We have been Beatles as best we ever will be—those four jolly lads. But we're not those people anymore."[1] Did this mean the band was breaking up? No one knew.

ON BREAK

Uncertain about whether the Beatles would work together again, Epstein felt lost and depressed. He used drugs more heavily,

The Beatles posed for photos at London's Heathrow Airport upon returning to England on August 31, 1966.

including sleeping pills, stimulants, and LSD. On September 30, 1966, newspapers reported that Epstein had been released from the hospital after being treated for glandular fever. This was not true. Epstein had taken an overdose of sleeping pills. It would not be his last attempt to take his own life.

Lennon flew to Germany to try his luck at acting. He had a small part in a film called *How I Won the War*. Often bored and high, he composed new music, including a deeply personal song called "Strawberry Fields Forever." When Lennon returned to England later that fall, he met someone who would help him understand himself better—Japanese artist Yoko Ono. She was in London to participate in a radical art movement that produced magazines, posters, concerts, and street theater designed to shock the public. Ono had an exhibition of her work in the Indica Gallery. Lennon was

Yoko Ono

Ono was one of the most experimental artists in Britain. When she first met Lennon in 1966 at the Indica Gallery, she handed him a card with only the word *breathe* written on it. Unsure of what to do, Lennon panted a bit. Then Ono took his arm and gave him a tour of the exhibit of her work. For her piece "Ceiling Painting," Ono had hung a canvas on the ceiling with one word written on it in minuscule writing. The viewer had to climb a ladder and use a magnifying glass to read the word *Yes*. Ono intrigued Lennon.

present when her exhibition was being installed, and her art intrigued him. After this meeting, Ono and Lennon kept in regular contact.

During the band's break, Starr focused on his family. In February 1965, he had married Maureen Cox, a fan who had asked for his autograph one day. By the fall of 1966, the couple had a son, and Starr was content to be home.

Harrison had married actress Patti Boyd in January 1966, and when the band went on break, the couple traveled to India so he could study sitar with a master. Six weeks of music, yoga, and meditation in the foothills of the Himalayas opened Harrison's mind to a new way of thinking. "It was the first feeling I've ever had," Harrison said, "of being liberated from [being] a Beatle."[2] He returned to London a changed man. His music was more focused, and his songwriting improved.

McCartney traveled to Europe and Africa during his time off. To avoid recognition, he grew a mustache, slicked back his hair, and wore fake glasses. This disguise made him invisible to Beatle fans, and he felt liberated.

On the flight home, McCartney drafted an idea for an album in which the Beatles would become a different band. When the flight attendant delivered McCartney's meal, McCartney noticed the salt and pepper packets labeled *S* and *P*. The image of an

Harrison and Boyd's trip to India changed the trajectory of Harrison's career.

old-fashioned bandleader sprang into McCartney's mind, and the name quickly followed: Sergeant Pepper. This name would lead to one of the Beatles' most iconic albums: *Sgt. Pepper's Lonely Hearts Club Band.*

SGT. PEPPER

On November 24, 1966, the Beatles gathered at Abbey Road Studios to begin making music again. John shared his dreamy, disjointed "Strawberry Fields Forever," and everyone loved it. George Martin called the song "a prototype for the future."[3]

As the band struggled to find a theme for the new album, McCartney shared the idea he had on the flight home. He suggested they make an entire album as though they were different people: the

Sgt. Pepper Cover

Pop artist Peter Blake created the album cover for *Sgt. Pepper's Lonely Hearts Club Band*. The Beatles, dressed in pink, blue, yellow, and scarlet uniforms, stand in front of a grave. Standing next to them are wax effigies of themselves. Also featured are a Buddha statue, a doll holding a sign that says "Welcome Rolling Stones," and images of celebrities including Marilyn Monroe, Bob Dylan, and Edgar Allan Poe. At first EMI rejected the cover, afraid the company would be sued by celebrities whose images were used. McCartney talked the company's president into allowing the cover. But EMI required the Beatles to take out 20 million pounds of insurance just in case. The insurance was never needed.

"If we felt at that time it was right to break a milk bottle over a cast-iron desk, record that sound, and multiply it, then we would have done it. We had no restrictions on our imaginations."[6]

– George Martin on making Sgt. Pepper's Lonely Hearts Club Band

"Changing the lifestyle and appearance of youth throughout the world didn't just happen—we set out to do it. We knew what we were doing."[7]

– John Lennon

Lonely Hearts Club Band led by Sgt. Pepper. Everyone was excited by the concept.

The masterpiece of *Sgt. Pepper's Lonely Hearts Club Band* was "A Day in the Life." Lennon wrote the beginning of a dark song inspired by the true story of a rich man who died in a car crash. However, he could not figure out how to end the song. Meanwhile, McCartney had written a song with a peppy beat about getting up late for work. They combined the songs, connecting them with the drawn-out cry, "I'd love to turn you on."[4]

Lennon wanted the song to have a grand finale like "a sound building up from nothing to the end of the world."[5] Martin figured out how to do it. He brought in a 41-piece orchestra but did not give them any music to play. Instead, Martin gave the orchestra a high note and a low note and told them to play anything in between. The result is a collision of sound that spirals until finally ending in a crashing piano chord.

Fans loved this new version of the Beatles. *Sgt. Pepper's Lonely Hearts Club Band* was released in June 1967. It took four months and 25,000 pounds to make, almost half a million dollars in 2020 currency. This was an unheard-of sum to produce an album at the time. But the album sold more than 2.5 million copies in only three months, topping charts in Britain for 27 weeks and in the United States for 15 weeks.[8]

Recording "A Day in the Life"

On February 10, 1967, the Beatles recorded the final version of "A Day in the Life" at the Abbey Road Studios. Guests included Mick Jagger and Keith Richards of the Rolling Stones and Michael Nesmith of the Monkees. The Beatles requested the 41-piece orchestra to wear evening dress, but then they gave the musicians funny disguises to wear. For example, the conductor wore a clown's red nose and a violinist wore a gorilla's paw. Despite the silliness, spectators knew they were witnessing something special. Sound engineer Tony Clark said, "I was speechless. The tempo changes—everything in that song—was just so dramatic and complete. I felt so privileged to be there."[9]

CHAPTER SEVEN

The Beatles Go It Alone

In the late 1960s, the Beatles began to search for deeper meaning in life, and they turned to Eastern philosophy for answers. When the Indian holy man Maharishi Mahesh Yogi spoke in London on August 24, 1967, George and Patti Harrison convinced Lennon and McCartney to attend the lecture with them. Mahesh had been visiting England for ten years. He claimed to know the secret to inner peace through a program he called Spiritual Regeneration.

Mahesh's message appealed to the Beatles, who were exhausted after years of making music and touring. After the lecture, Lennon, McCartney, and Harrison introduced

The Beatles' time with Maharishi Mahesh Yogi exposed them to new kinds of philosophy.

themselves to the holy man and said they wanted to learn more. Mahesh invited them to attend his summer conference in Wales that started in two days.

Last Beatle to Marry

In 1967, McCartney met American photographer Linda Eastman at a London nightclub. They met again four days later when Linda photographed the launch for the *Sgt. Pepper* album. However, at the time, McCartney was in a long-term relationship with a British actress. Eventually, that relationship ended, and McCartney and Eastman reconnected again in the United States in the spring of 1968. Three months later, he asked Eastman to move to England, and she agreed. The couple married on March 12, 1969.

THE LOSS OF BRIAN EPSTEIN

The band members invited Epstein to join them at the conference, but Epstein said he had other plans that weekend. It was odd for the band to travel without its manager. He had looked after the Beatles on every trip the band had taken for the last five years.

The Beatles arrived in Wales on Saturday, August 26, and were housed in a former teachers' college with 300 other conference attendees. The band embraced Mahesh's life philosophy quickly. The day after they arrived, all four Beatles held a press conference during which McCartney announced the Beatles were renouncing drugs. "It's an experience we went through," he said. "We don't need it anymore."[1]

While the Beatles were reshaping their inner selves, Epstein was wrestling with his. On the night of August 27, he died from an accidental overdose. It was believed that he had taken pills to fall asleep, then woke in the night, and without thinking, took more. Mixed with the alcohol Epstein had consumed that day, the drugs were fatal.

News that their friend and manager was dead stunned the Beatles. Epstein had steered their rise from a small-time Liverpool band to a global sensation. The Beatles immediately returned to London.

The Beatles not only had to deal with the loss of their friend but they also had business affairs dumped in their laps. Epstein had died without a will, so his estate was taken over by his younger brother Clive. The Beatles agreed to accept Clive Epstein as their temporary manager until the contract they had with NEMS ended in two months. However, Clive had no experience in managing a band, so the Beatles had

> "Even in the last year of Brian's life they were beginning to go their separate ways. . . . After he died obviously the Beatles wanted to develop in their separate and individual ways."[2]
>
> – *Clive Epstein*

to figure things out themselves. It was a steep learning curve.

MAGICAL MYSTERY TOUR

McCartney proposed the next project. He had written a song called "Magical Mystery Tour" and suggested they rent a bus and go on a tour around the English countryside. They could film the journey, directing the project themselves. The idea of having total control excited all four Beatles.

The bus set off in September 1967, but there was little mystery involved. With the slogan "Magical Mystery Tour" painted on the sides of the bus, the band could not travel undetected. Media and fans trailed the Beatles everywhere. Details Brian Epstein had previously handled, such as hotel registration, permits, and traffic jams, were now the Beatles' burdens. The band members hired numerous extras to appear during the tour, but they had not written a script, so the actors did not know what to do. The Beatles did not give any directions to the cameramen either. The tour was more chaos than mystery.

After 11 weeks of editing, the BBC eventually bought the movie. *Magical Mystery Tour* was broadcast on December 26, 1967. The 15 million Brits who tuned in to see the Beatles were largely disappointed. The film was clumsy and crude. The

The Beatles aboard a bus during the filming of *Magical Mystery Tour* in September 1967

Beatles were only visible through the bus windows or dressed up in strange costumes. For the first time in years, the Beatles found themselves criticized everywhere. They knew that if Epstein were alive, he would never have allowed them to release such a poor film.

BEATLES AS BUSINESSMEN

The Beatles earned a lot of money, but they did not get to keep most of it. The tax rate in Britain was as high as 98 percent for the highest earners.

Yellow Submarine

The Beatles' fourth film was *Yellow Submarine*, a cartoon. The Beatles only made the movie to fulfill a contractual obligation and were not enthusiastic about it. However, when the film opened in London on July 17, 1968, it was a hit. The cartoon was a fantasy about a world called Pepperland and villains called the Blue Meanies. Four little cartoon Beatles floated through the movie with childlike innocence.

Accountants advised the band to invest in music-related businesses to get some tax breaks.

In January 1968, the Beatles formed the holding company Apple Corps Ltd. A holding company buys shares of other companies and then controls them. The first company Apple Corps formed was a new partnership called Beatles and Co. The corporation controlled 80 percent of the partnership, and each Beatle owned another five percent. The corporation's money was combined into a common pot, and decisions could be passed with a majority vote by the four band members. These rules seemed fine at the time, but they would cause serious problems for the band later.

Apple Corps launched several offshoot businesses, including a boutique, an electronics company, an arts foundation, and Apple Records, a record and film company. It was Apple Records that showed the most initial success. The Beatles wanted to help future artists get a start. So they placed advertisements in music magazines urging people to send in tapes of their songs and ideas for films.

Apple Corps's headquarters was on a London property that the Beatles' accountants purchased as an investment. Artists, writers, and musicians seeking funding swarmed the house, but the Beatles had no business plan. Soon money was flowing out of Apple Corps much faster than it was coming in.

Losing Money

In the words of McCartney, the mission of Apple Corps was to establish "a business with a social and cultural environment where everyone gets a decent share of the profits."[3] But no one working for Apple Corps had any business experience, and each venture became a money pit. Customers walked out of Apple Boutique without paying for merchandise. Apple's accountants received astronomical bills for imported vodka and caviar from the company's London building, which became much better known for its extravagant parties than its business meetings.

After months of working on Apple Corps, the Beatles decided to return to making music. But when they arrived at Abbey Road on May 30, 1968, to start on a new album, the Beatles discovered new tensions in their working relationships—tensions that would ultimately tear the band apart.

CHAPTER EIGHT

The Breakup

In May 1968, the Beatles gathered at Abbey Road Studios to begin collaboration on a new album called *The Beatles*, often referred to as *The White Album* for its blank, white cover. Almost immediately, relationships that had been strained for the past year began to fray.

YOKO ONO IN THE STUDIO

Lennon arrived with Yoko Ono on his arm. Although John and Cynthia Lennon would not divorce until November 1968, John and Ono had become a couple the previous year. The Beatles never let anyone other than

Lennon's relationship with Yoko Ono, *left*, was just one of many factors that created tension within the band in 1968.

Martin remain in the studio during recording, but now Ono sat by Lennon's side.

Lennon expected the rest of the band to accept Ono's presence, but the other three Beatles did not. The first time Ono spoke up to give Lennon advice on his singing, McCartney erupted: "Did somebody speak? Who . . . was that? Did you say something, George?"[1] In a 1970 interview, Lennon told a reporter about the time Harrison told Ono that "she gave off bad vibes."[2] Years later, Lennon still seethed at the memory.

Ono's art and personality had opened up a new perspective for Lennon. When his bandmates rejected her, he realized, "I could no longer artistically get anything out of the Beatles and here was someone that could turn me on to a million things."[3] So Lennon and Ono began to record music together, and he began to pull away from the Beatles.

RUPTURED RELATIONSHIPS

The Beatles began to work individually, each man guarding his own material closely. Martin said he was not recording a band but three different guitar players and singers. "George would do his own thing and the others would join in, a little more reluctantly than they used to. And Paul would do his own thing and sometimes John wouldn't turn up."[4]

The tension took a toll on Starr. Halfway through the recording of *The Beatles*, he snapped. Explaining that he was playing badly, Starr quit the band. However, the other Beatles did not think he was serious. They were right. After a week at home, Starr returned to Abbey Road. McCartney and Harrison welcomed him back by covering his drum set with messages and flowers.

The Beatles was released on November 22, 1968. Although the album has no unifying theme and was really a collection of solo tracks, it wowed fans and critics. *Rolling Stone* magazine called it "the best album they [the Beatles] have ever released."[5] The *Sunday Times* said the album had "beauty, horror, surprise, chaos, order. And that is the world; and that is what the Beatles are on about."[6]

Paul Is Dead?

On October 12, 1969, a caller phoned Detroit disc jockey Russ Gibb and told him to play "Revolution 9" from *The Beatles* backward. When Gibb did, he heard the words "Turn me on, dead man." From then on, a conspiracy theory spread that McCartney had died in a car accident in 1966 and the band had replaced him with an impostor. Fans found supposed clues in song lyrics and on album covers. Meanwhile, McCartney was living quietly in Scotland.

THE STRUGGLE TO MAKE *LET IT BE*

Following the release of *The Beatles*, McCartney urged the band to do a live show to reconnect with fans, but Harrison refused. Instead, the Beatles decided to make their next album more like a live performance by not using technology to transform songs. Recording sessions would be filmed, and the Beatles would turn this footage into a movie, its climax a brief live performance.

Rehearsals started on January 2, 1969. McCartney tried to keep everyone on task, but his schoolteacher manner irritated his bandmates. "Paul would want us to work all the time," said Starr, "because he was the workaholic."[7] When McCartney instructed Harrison on how to play the guitar, Harrison shut down. Martin admitted McCartney could be "rather overbossy," but he said it was the only way the band got any work done.[8]

Then on January 10, Harrison and Lennon got in a serious fight. Harrison packed up his guitar and said, "I'm out of here. Put an ad in [the papers]. . . . See you 'round the clubs."[9] McCartney and Starr were shocked, but Lennon shrugged and suggested they hire star guitarist Eric Clapton to replace Harrison.

A few days later, the Beatles hashed out their differences. McCartney promised to stop criticizing

Harrison's playing, while Lennon demanded that Ono be allowed to attend all recording sessions. "She wants to be one of us," he said.[10] Starr replied, "She's not a Beatle, John, and she never will be."[11] Lennon refused to give in. If the Beatles wanted him, they had to accept Ono. They agreed, and everyone returned to the studio.

The Fifth Beatle

The Beatles met American musician Billy Preston in Hamburg, Germany, in 1962. Harrison brought Preston to the studio during recording for *Let It Be*, and for ten days, Preston played keyboard with the band. He brought new energy and professionalism to the group when it desperately needed it. With Preston around, the Beatles were polite and performed better. Lennon liked Preston so much he wanted to make him the fifth Beatle, but McCartney said, "It's bad enough with four."[12] However, Preston's name was listed on the Beatles single "Get Back." He was the first musician outside the group to get this recognition.

The album that emerged was *Let It Be*. The Beatles recorded more than 100 songs while working on the project, only a fraction of which were used on the final album. All that was left was to record the movie's grand finale: the live concert. Harrison still refused to perform at large-scale venues. Instead, on the afternoon of January 30, 1969, the Beatles performed on the roof of the Apple Corps building.

The only witnesses were the Beatles' employees and a few close friends. People on the street below

The rooftop concert became a legendary moment in the band's history.

stopped in wonder. They could hear the Beatles but not see them. Finally, after traffic came to a standstill, a police officer ordered a halt to the music. At the end of the concert, Lennon said,

"I'd like to say thank you . . . and I hope we passed the audition."[13] It was the last time all four Beatles played together in public.

The band still needed to edit its recordings and select 14 songs to be featured on *Let It Be*. But the workload was immense, and the recording sessions had been so negative that none of the Beatles could stomach the job. So the tapes lay abandoned in the studio.

MONEY AND MANAGERS

By 1969, the Beatles' finances were a mess. The companies owned by Apple Corps were losing money, and each Beatle had borrowed heavily from the corporation. In October, their accountant resigned. He said if the Beatles did not cut costs, they faced bankruptcy.

> "You were never concerned where the money came from or how it was being spent, and were living under the idea that you had millions at your disposal."[14]
>
> *– Beatles accountant Stephen Maltz in his resignation letter, October 1969*

The band argued over whom it could hire to dig it out of financial trouble. McCartney suggested the father and brother of Linda Eastman, then his girlfriend and later his wife. They were New York attorneys. But Lennon wanted to hire New York accountant Allen Klein. Although Klein was known as a good negotiator, he also had a reputation for shady business dealings. When the other Beatles met Klein,

Harrison and Starr were willing to sign with him. McCartney was not.

Finally, in the spring of 1969, Lennon, Harrison, and Starr signed with Klein. He served as the Beatles' manager while the band produced its final album. However, McCartney never signed the contract. That fact would become very important later.

ABBEY ROAD IS THE END OF THE ROAD

The Beatles' final album was *Abbey Road.* McCartney and Martin envisioned an album that was one continuous movement of music as each song rolled into the next. But Lennon wanted to play plain old rock and roll.

Ultimately, they compromised. One side of the record was a collection of individual songs, and the other side formed a continuous piece. The song lyrics hinted at the mood of the Beatles during this final summer. In "Come Together," Lennon wrote that "you've got to be free," and McCartney wrote a song titled "The End." Harrison contributed "Something" and "Here Comes the Sun," two of the best-received songs on the album.

In September 1969, two weeks before *Abbey Road* was released, Lennon and Ono performed at the Toronto Rock and Roll Revival. The experience

Going Cold Turkey

The Beatles were no strangers to drugs. During their Hamburg days, they took amphetamines. During the filming of *Help!*, they smoked marijuana, and *Sgt. Pepper* was heavily influenced by their experimentation with LSD. However, the heaviest drug user was Lennon, who became addicted to heroin in early 1969. In the fall of 1969, Lennon decided to get sober, a struggle he recounted in the song "Cold Turkey."

convinced Lennon that he no longer needed the Beatles. A week later, McCartney once again encouraged the band to perform live. Lennon told him, "I think you're daft. I wasn't going to tell you, but I'm breaking the group up. It feels good. It feels like a divorce."[15]

McCartney, Harrison, and Starr were stunned. Klein convinced Lennon not to announce his decision publicly yet. He had just negotiated a better royalty deal with EMI and did not want to spook company executives. In addition, no one was sure whether Lennon's decision was permanent.

However, Lennon's announcement shattered McCartney. He had been a Beatle since he was 15 and could not imagine a future without the band. He spiraled into a depression. By this time, McCartney was married to Eastman, and she urged him to get out of his funk by making new music. In December, McCartney started working on a solo album. A few months later, he called Lennon

The simple, iconic cover of *Abbey Road* showed the band members walking through a crosswalk outside the studio.

and said he was leaving the Beatles too. "Good," Lennon said. "That makes two of us who have accepted it mentally."[16]

THE FANS FIND OUT

It was McCartney who told the public the Beatles were splitting up, but he did this only after he felt the band had betrayed him. The recordings for *Let It Be* were collecting dust in the basement of the Apple Corps building, waiting to be edited. None of the band members wanted to do the job, so in

March 1970, Lennon asked music producer Phil Spector to take on the task. Without McCartney's permission, Spector made major changes to "Let It Be" and "The Long and Winding Road," two songs McCartney wrote. He hated the changes and asked for revisions. Klein refused.

McCartney's debut solo album was scheduled for release in mid-April 1970. A week before its launch, McCartney released promotional materials that included a series of questions and answers. One question was, "Do you foresee a time when Lennon/McCartney becomes an active songwriting partnership again?" McCartney's answer was "No."[17] That one word told the world the Beatles were over. Fans were devastated.

> "You can imagine what I had to go through, suing my best mates. . . . knowing that no one would understand it."[18]
>
> *– Paul McCartney*

THE FINAL STEP

McCartney wanted to sever all financial relationships with the Beatles. However, Lennon and Harrison refused to release him from the Apple Corps partnership. So on December 31, 1970, McCartney sued in court. Because McCartney had never signed the contract with Klein, the judge ruled in McCartney's favor. Although the process took a few years, this final step formally dissolved the Beatles.

Music critics and fans argue about what broke up the Beatles. Personality clashes between Lennon and McCartney? Financial stress or the simple fact that four old friends had outgrown their musical relationship? Likely, it was a combination of multiple factors. Whatever the cause, the result was indisputable: the Beatles would never make music together again.

CHAPTER NINE

"Messengers from the Universe"

John, Paul, George, and Ringo all pursued solo careers. Over the next few decades, each released new albums with new bands as backup. Each man had some success, but none achieved the legacy left by the Beatles.

Lennon had already recorded three albums with Ono before the Beatles' official split. He continued this work after the band broke up. Lennon's fans were not keen on his new style. He recorded an album every year through 1975, but only *Imagine*, released in 1971, sold well.

Lennon and Ono moved to New York City. They had a son, and Lennon devoted

Lennon spent time after the Beatles collaborating with Ono on music and advocacy for world peace.

himself to being a full-time parent. This experience mellowed him. McCartney and Lennon did not fully reconcile, though they did begin to repair their friendship.

To John, Love Paul

In 1994, the Rock & Roll Hall of Fame gave the late Lennon a lifetime achievement award. At the event, McCartney gave a speech that was a love letter to his old friend. After tracing the highlights of their long relationship, McCartney ended by saying, "Thank you, for everything. . . . This letter comes with love from your friend, Paul. John Lennon, you made it. Tonight you're in the Rock 'n Roll Hall of Fame."[2]

Lennon began to compose again, but this time he sang about being a father and a husband. On November 17, 1980, Lennon and Ono released *Double Fantasy*. It did not sell well, but Lennon did not despair. He told reporters, "Life begins at forty, so they promise. And I believe it, too. . . . I'm, like, excited. . . . What's going to happen next?"[1]

On the night of December 8, 1980, Lennon and Ono returned to their apartment from the recording studio. Lennon was heading for the door of the building when 25-year-old Mark David Chapman, a fan with mental health problems, stepped out of the shadows and shot five bullets into Lennon's back. Lennon died before he reached the hospital.

Beatles fans around the world were devastated. The gates around Lennon's New York apartment became a memorial, and candlelight vigils were held in Los Angeles and Washington, DC.

RINGO STILL A STAR

Initially, it appeared that Starr would have the most successful solo career. He put out two hugely successful singles: "It Don't Come Easy," which topped the charts in 1971, and "Back Off Boogaloo," in 1972. His 1973 album, *Ringo*, gave the singer two Number 1 hits in the United States, "Photograph" and "You're Sixteen." Starr also appeared in a couple of movies and even directed one.

However, by the mid-1970s, Starr's music began to sound stale. His songs no longer broke into the charts. Starr worked playing drums for other artists, including Bob Dylan and Tom Petty, and also became a voice actor.

Still a Star

In 2015, Starr was inducted into the Rock & Roll Hall of Fame, the last Beatle to get that honor. Fans felt this recognition had been denied for too long. When asked what this meant to him, Starr said, "It means recognition. And it means, finally, the four of us are in the Rock and Roll Hall of Fame even though we were the biggest pop group in the land."[3]

In the 2000s, Starr went on tour two to three times a year and

Starr found success touring alongside other artists.

planned to continue this as long as he could. He remained friends with the other Beatles, who all played on his solo albums and wrote songs for him. This was natural because to Starr, the Beatles were "just four guys who loved each other."[4]

FINDING PEACE

For many years, Harrison resented playing second fiddle to Lennon and McCartney. After the band's breakup, he was free to shine on his own. Harrison's first solo album, *All Things Must Pass*, was released in November 1970. The three-record set was proof of Harrison's creativity, and the track "My Sweet Lord" reached Number 1.

However, the success of "My Sweet Lord" suffered when a judge ruled that Harrison had "unconsciously plagiarized" the song's three-note hook from the 1963 hit "He's So Fine" by the Chiffons.[5] After this, Harrison did not have any hit singles, and his reputation as a solo artist diminished.

Harrison was a heavy smoker, and in March 2001, cancer was discovered in one of his lungs. He began to put his affairs in order, including repairing his relationship with McCartney. In the fall of 2001, as Harrison was undergoing radiation therapy, McCartney visited Harrison. They agreed that their long-ago squabbles mattered little in the end. Harrison died on November 29, 2001.

Remembering George

On the one-year anniversary of Harrison's death, a memorial concert in his honor was held at London's Royal Albert Hall. The star-studded event featured some of rock's greatest musicians who had also been Harrison's friends. These included the last remaining Beatles—McCartney and Starr. Then, on March 15, 2004, Harrison was inducted into the Rock & Roll Hall of Fame. During the ceremony, an all-star cast of guitarists played "While My Guitar Gently Weeps," Harrison's most famous Beatles song.

Harrison plays guitar on a 1974 solo-tour stop in Maryland.

SOARING SOLO

In 1971, McCartney formed a new band—Wings. The group got little attention at first. So McCartney started over at the bottom again. The band packed its equipment into a van and went on the road, playing small halls and clubs. In 1972, McCartney wrote the title song for the James Bond film *Live and Let Die*, and it became a Top 10 hit. That success was followed in 1973 by the top-selling album *Band on the Run*.

Throughout the 1970s, Wings drew large crowds. After McCartney was arrested in Tokyo in 1980 for possession of marijuana, Wings broke up, and McCartney retreated from public life. He reemerged in the late 1990s, and since then he has put out albums and toured annually.

LEGACY

The Beatles launched a revolution in music and in society. One way the Beatles changed music was to popularize the sound of rock and roll music played on multiple electric guitars. The electric guitar was not mass-produced until the 1950s, so the Beatles were part of the first generation that could afford one. According to Michael Tomsky, author of *Yeah! Yeah! Yeah!: The Beatles and America, Then and Now*, the Beatles were the first band to incorporate influences from R&B, country, Broadway, and pop into music played by multiple guitars at high volume. This became the classic sound of rock and roll.

Another musical legacy of the Beatles was their willingness to experiment and evolve. This experimentation was encouraged by producer George Martin. The Beatles used synthesizers, recorded tapes in reverse, and played unusual instruments to create new and interesting sounds. Martin recognized the Beatles' greatness. After the

McCartney, *right*, maintained a busy touring schedule well into his seventies.

band broke up, he reflected, "Whether we will ever see another group like the Beatles is impossible to say, but I should think it very unlikely."[6]

Although the Beatles broke up in 1970, their fans remain a global community. Fans make pilgrimages to Liverpool and Abbey Road. They analyze and interpret Beatles lyrics in online communities. Fans report the pleasure they feel at introducing their grandchildren to the Beatles' music. In this manner, the phenomenon that was the Beatles is transmitted to a new generation. One fan described John, Paul, George, and Ringo as "messengers from the universe."[7] As long as their music survives, the Beatles' message will last forever.

"When I think about them, it's more like a feeling of wonder. I wonder how all of us were so lucky that something as great as the Beatles occurred in our lifetime."[8]

– A 49-year-old Beatles' fan quoted in Beatleness: How the Beatles and Their Fans Remade the World

TIMELINE

1956

John Lennon and some high school friends form a band called the Quarrymen.

1957

On July 6, Lennon and Paul McCartney meet for the first time at a festival in Woolton, England, and shortly after Lennon invites McCartney to join his band.

1958

Lennon agrees to let 15-year-old George Harrison join the Quarrymen.

1960

By August, the band has changed its name to the Beatles; it hires Pete Best as drummer ahead of shows that month in Hamburg, Germany.

1961

The Beatles make their first single, playing backup for singer Tony Sheridan; in December, the Beatles sign a contract with agent Brian Epstein.

1962

In June, the Beatles audition for producer George Martin of Parlophone Records, an imprint of EMI; a few weeks later, the band fires Best and hires Ringo Starr.

1964

On February 1, "I Want to Hold Your Hand" reaches Number 1 on the US *Billboard* charts; on February 9, the Beatles perform on the *Ed Sullivan Show* for the first time; on July 6, the Beatles' film *A Hard Day's Night* premieres in London.

1965

In August, the film *Help!* hits the theaters.

1966

In August, *Revolver* is released, representing the beginning of the Beatles' experimental music phase.

1967

In June, *Sgt. Pepper's Lonely Hearts Club Band* is released; on August 27, Epstein dies from an accidental overdose of sleeping pills.

1968

In January, the Beatles form Apple Corps Ltd.; on November 22, *The Beatles* is released.

1969

On January 30, the Beatles perform publicly together for the last time, on the roof of the Apple Corps building.

1970

In April, McCartney releases publicity materials for his solo debut that reveal to the public that the Beatles have broken up.

1980

Lennon is shot and killed on December 8.

2001

Harrison dies on November 29 after battling cancer.

ESSENTIAL FACTS

Beatles Band Members

- **John Lennon** was the founding member of the Quarrymen in 1956, the band that eventually became the Beatles. He sang lead vocals, played guitar, and composed many Beatles songs until the band broke up in 1970.
- **Paul McCartney** was invited to join the Quarrymen by John Lennon in 1957 and remained with the Beatles until 1970. He shared the role of lead vocalist with Lennon. McCartney played guitar and wrote many Beatles songs.
- **George Harrison** was invited to join the Quarrymen in 1958 and remained with the Beatles until 1970. He sang backup vocals and played guitar, bass, sitar, and keyboards.
- **Pete Best** joined the Beatles as a drummer in 1960 but was fired in 1962, just before the band recorded its first record with a major label.
- **Richard Starkey**, also known as **Ringo Starr**, played percussion with the band Rory Storm and the Hurricanes before Lennon, McCartney, and Harrison recruited him to replace Best as drummer for the Beatles. He sang vocals and played drums and keyboards as a Beatle until 1970.

Beatles Studio Albums

- *Please Please Me* (1963)
- *With the Beatles* (1963)
- *A Hard Day's Night* (1964)
- *Beatles for Sale* (1964)
- *Help* (1965)
- *Rubber Soul* (1965)
- *Revolver* (1966)

- *Sgt. Pepper's Lonely Hearts Club Band* (1967)
- *The Beatles [The White Album]* (1968)
- *Yellow Submarine* (1969)
- *Abbey Road* (1969)
- *Let It Be* (1970)

Career Highlights

The Beatles are the most iconic rock band of all time. They began their career playing mostly teenage rock and roll love songs, but the band members later expanded their horizons with new lyrical themes and innovative music-production techniques. The band was an immense cultural force at its peak in the late 1960s, selling millions of albums and influencing popular culture. The Beatles' breakup in 1970 was international news.

Conflicts

Personality clashes, differences in working style, and financial disagreements contributed to the breakup of the Beatles. Paul McCartney sued to have the Beatles' financial partnership dissolved, and the court ruled in his favor.

Quote

"Now what happened with the Beatles was that they were the first real group where there was no one single individual who was the center of attention. . . . Suddenly you had a four-piece band that played their own instruments . . . and America was ready for them."

—Cliff Richards, British pop star

GLOSSARY

accountant
A person whose job it is to manage a company's financial accounts.

audition
An interview for a job where a singer or dancer performs his or her skill.

compose
To write or create new music.

counterculture
A culture of values that go against those of established society, popularized in the 1960s.

dissolve
To cancel a contract or legal relationship between parties.

documentary
A nonfiction movie that presents a factual record of events.

embassy
The official place in a foreign country where an ambassador works to represent his or her country.

experimentation
Trying out new ideas, methods, or activities.

gig
A job for a musician, actor, or other performer.

liberate
To set free.

manager
In music, a person who guides a musician's career.

phenomenon
A very big deal.

picket
To stand outside a place to protest something.

pompadour
A man's hairstyle in which the front of the hair is brushed up from the forehead into a high mound.

record label
A company that promotes and publishes a band's music.

royalty
A share of money generated by sales of a work.

skiffle
A kind of folk music with a blues or jazz influence, played by a small group, that often used improvised musical instruments, such as washboards.

symbolize
To represent something else.

track
A song or piece of music recorded onto a physical medium.

ADDITIONAL RESOURCES

Selected Bibliography

The Beatles: Ten Years That Shook the World. DK, 2004.

Davies, Hunter. *The Beatles*. Norton, 2010.

Norman, Philip. *Shout! The Beatles in Their Generation*. Simon & Schuster, 2005.

Pritchard, David, and Alan Lysaght. *The Beatles: An Oral History*. Hyperion, 1998.

Further Readings

Asher, Peter. *The Beatles from A to Zed: An Alphabetical Mystery Tour*. Henry Holt, 2019.

Pring, John, and Rob Thomas. *Visualizing the Beatles: A Complete Graphic History of the World's Favorite Band*. Dey St., 2018.

Sheffield, Rob. *Dreaming the Beatles: The Love Story of One Band and the Whole World*. Dey St., 2018.

Online Resources

To learn more about the Beatles, please visit **abdobooklinks.com** or scan this QR code. These links are routinely monitored and updated to provide the most current information available.

More Information

For more information on this subject, contact or visit the following organizations:

Abbey Road Studios
3 Abbey Rd.
St. John's Wood, London NW8 9AY
England
+44 0 20 7266 7000
abbeyroad.com

This music studio was made famous because it is where most Beatles songs were recorded. Abbey Road remains a functioning recording studio today. Visitors can stride the crosswalk that was immortalized on the cover of the Abbey Road album, write on the graffiti wall, and visit the Abbey Road Shop.

Cavern Club and Magical Mystery Tour
10 Mathew St.
Liverpool L2 6RE
England
+44 0 151 703 9100
cavernclub.com/tour-enquiries/

Join a two-hour Magical Mystery Tour to see all the Beatles sites in Liverpool, England, including the Beatles' childhood homes and schools and places made famous in their songs, such as Penny Lane and the Strawberry Fields. The tour ends at the Cavern Club, where audiences can still enjoy live music.

SOURCE NOTES

CHAPTER 1. LADIES AND GENTLEMEN, THE BEATLES!

1. Richard Corliss. "Like Yesterday: America Meets the Beatles." *Time*, 7 Feb. 2014, entertainment.time.com. Accessed 9 Mar. 2020.

2. "How the Beatles Took America." *Rolling Stone*, 1 Jan. 2014, rollingstone.com. Accessed 9 Mar. 2020.

3. Philip Norman. *Shout! The Beatles in their Generation.* Fireside, 2003. 246.

4. "How the Beatles Took America."

5. Norman, *Shout! The Beatles in their Generation*, 246.

6. Norman, *Shout! The Beatles in their Generation*, 247.

7. Norman, *Shout! The Beatles in their Generation*, 248.

8. Norman, *Shout! The Beatles in their Generation*, 252.

9. Norman, *Shout! The Beatles in their Generation*, 247.

10. Norman, *Shout! The Beatles in their Generation*, 252.

11. Jim Sullivan. "The Beatles' American Invasion." *U.S. News Digital Weekly*, Jan. 2014, connection.ebscohost.com. Accessed 9 Mar. 2020.

12. Norman, *Shout! The Beatles in their Generation*, 251.

13. Norman, *Shout! The Beatles in their Generation*, 251.

14. Norman, *Shout! The Beatles in their Generation*, 251.

15. "How the Beatles Took America."

16. David Pritchard and Alan Lysaght. *Beatles: An Oral History.* Hyperion, 1998. 151.

17. "How the Beatles Took America."

18. Paul Trynka. *The Beatles.* Dorling Kindersley, 2004. 105.

19. Pritchard and Lysaght, *Beatles: An Oral History*, 147.

CHAPTER 2. THE BEGINNING

1. Mark Lewisohn. *The Beatles: All These Years.* Crown Archetype, 2013. 88.

2. Philip Norman. *Shout! The Beatles in their Generation.* Fireside, 2003. 25.

3. Mark Lewisohn. "How John Lennon Buried his Mother in Song." *Newsweek*, 20 Jan. 2014, newsweek.com. Accessed 9 Mar. 2020.

4. Hunter Davies. *The Beatles.* Norton, 2010. 31.

5. Davies, *The Beatles*, 32.

6. Davies, *The Beatles*, 25.

7. Davies, *The Beatles*, 39.

8. Davies, *The Beatles*, 76.

9. David Pritchard and Alan Lysaght. *Beatles: An Oral History.* Hyperion, 1998. 42.

CHAPTER 3. BRITISH BEATLEMANIA

1. Hunter Davies. *The Beatles.* Norton, 2010. 92.
2. *The Beatles Anthology*. Chronicle Books, 2000. 57.
3. Davies, *The Beatles*, 124.
4. Davies, *The Beatles*, 124.
5. Davies, *The Beatles*, 135.
6. Davies, *The Beatles*, 137.
7. Davies, *The Beatles*, 151.
8. Davies, *The Beatles*, 137–138.
9. Jordan Runtagh. "10 Great Beatles Moments We Owe to George Martin." *Rolling Stone*, 9 Mar. 2016, rollingstone.com. Accessed 9 Mar. 2020.
10. Dorian Lynskey. "Beatlemania: 'The Screamers' And Other Tales of Fandom." *Guardian*, 28 Sept. 2013, theguardian.com. Accessed 9 Mar. 2020.

CHAPTER 4. US INVASION

1. Philip Norman. *Shout! The Beatles in their Generation.* Fireside, 2003. 225.
2. Norman, *Shout! The Beatles in their Generation*, 227.
3. "How the Beatles Took America." *Rolling Stone*, 1 Jan. 2014, rollingstone.com. Accessed 9 Mar. 2020.
4. Ian MacDonald. "How 'I Want to Hold Your Hand' Revolutionized Pop." *Slate*. 11 Nov. 2013, slate.com. Accessed 9 Mar. 2020.
5. "How the Beatles Took America."
6. Ian McDonald. "The Beatles Race Around the Clock." *Slate*, 25 Feb. 2013, slate.com. Accessed 9 Mar. 2020.
7. Jim Sullivan. "What the Beatles Meant to America." *U.S. News*, 21 Jan. 2014, usnews.com. Accessed 8 Oct. 2019.
8. Sullivan, "What the Beatles Meant to America."
9. Paul Trynka. *The Beatles.* Dorling Kindersley, 2004. 144.
10. "How the Beatles Took America."

CHAPTER 5. MAKING MOVIES AND TOURING THE WORLD

1. Paul Trynka. *The Beatles.* Dorling Kindersley, 2004. 162.
2. David Pritchard and Alan Lysaght. *Beatles: An Oral History.* Hyperion, 1998. 201.
3. Mikal Gilmore. "Beatles' Acid Test." *Rolling Stone*, 25 Aug. 2016, rollingstone.com. Accessed 10 Oct. 2019.
4. Trynka, *The Beatles*, 211.
5. Pritchard and Lysaght, *Beatles: An Oral History*, 229.

SOURCE NOTES CONTINUED

CHAPTER 6. EXPERIMENTATION

1. Steve Turner. *Beatles 66: The Revolutionary Year.* Harper Collins, 2016. 316.
2. Paul Trynka. *The Beatles*. Dorling Kindersley, 2004. 232.
3. Mikal Gilmore. "Inside the Making of 'Sgt. Pepper.'" *Rolling Stone*, 1 June 2017, rollingstone.com. Accessed 30 Oct. 2019.
4. Philip Norman. *Shout! The Beatles in their Generation.* Fireside, 2003. 328.
5. Norman, *Shout! The Beatles in their Generation*, 328.
6. David Pritchard and Alan Lysaght. *Beatles: An Oral History.* Hyperion, 1998. 248.
7. Gilmore, "Inside the Making of 'Sgt. Pepper.'"
8. Olivia B. Waxman. "The Story Behind the Sgt. Pepper's Lonely Hearts Club Band Album Cover." *Time*, 30 Mar. 2017, time.com. Accessed 11 Oct. 2019.
9. "Recording: A Day in the Life." *The Beatles Bible*, 10 Feb. 1967, beatlesbible.com. Accessed 12 Oct. 2019.

CHAPTER 7. THE BEATLES GO IT ALONE

1. Philip Norman. *Shout! The Beatles in their Generation.* Fireside, 2003. 343.
2. David Pritchard and Alan Lysaght. *Beatles: An Oral History.* Hyperion, 1998. 255.
3. "Apple - The Short, Strange Blossoming of The Beatles' Dream." *Independent*, 22 Oct. 2010, independent.co.uk. Accessed 14 Oct. 2019.

CHAPTER 8. THE BREAKUP

1. Mikal Gilmore. "Why the Beatles Broke Up." *Rolling Stone*, 3 Sept. 2009, rollingstone.com. Accessed 17 Oct. 2019.
2. Jann S. Wenner. "Lennon Remembers, Part One." *Rolling Stone*, 21 Jan. 1971, rollingstone.com. Accessed 18 Oct. 2019.
3. Wenner, "Lennon Remembers, Part One."
4. David Pritchard and Alan Lysaght. *Beatles: An Oral History.* Hyperion, 1998. 263.
5. Wenner, "Lennon Remembers, Part One."
6. Paul Trynka. *The Beatles.* Dorling Kindersley, 2004. 342.
7. Gilmore, "Why the Beatles Broke Up."

8. Gilmore, "Why the Beatles Broke Up."
9. Gilmore, "Why the Beatles Broke Up."
10. Gilmore, "Why the Beatles Broke Up."
11. Gilmore, "Why the Beatles Broke Up."
12. Gilmore, "Why the Beatles Broke Up."
13. Marisa Iati. "The Beatles Played on a London Rooftop in 1969. It Wound up Being Their Last Show." *Washington Post*, 30 Jan. 2019, washingtonpost.com. Accessed 18 Oct. 2019.
14. Philip Norman. *Shout! The Beatles in Their Generation*. Simon & Schuster, 2005. 399.
15. Gilmore, "Why the Beatles Broke Up."
16. Gilmore, "Why the Beatles Broke Up."
17. Gilmore, "Why the Beatles Broke Up."
18. Trynka, *The Beatles*, 433.

CHAPTER 9. "MESSENGERS FROM THE UNIVERSE"

1. Philip Norman. *Shout! The Beatles in their Generation*. Simon & Schuster, 2005. 467.
2. "Paul McCartney Inducts John Lennon into the Rock and Roll Hall of Fame." *YouTube*, uploaded by Rock & Roll Hall of Fame, 23 Nov. 2011, youtube.com. Accessed 20 Oct. 2019.
3. Andy Greene. "Ringo Starr on Hall of Fame Induction." *Rolling Stone*, 16 Dec. 2014, rollingstone.com. Accessed 20 Oct. 2019.
4. Norman, *Shout! The Beatles in their Generation*, 525.
5. Adam Bernstein. "Beatles' George Harrison Dies." *Washington Post*, 1 Dec. 2001, washingtonpost.com. Accessed 8 Dec. 2019.
6. David Pritchard and Alan Lysaght. *Beatles: An Oral History*. Hyperion, 1998. 320.
7. Norman, *Shout! The Beatles in their Generation*, 484.
8. Candy Leonard. *Beatleness: How The Beatles and Their Fans Remade The World*. Arcade Publishing, 2014. 273.

INDEX

ABOUT THE AUTHOR

Judy Dodge Cummings

Judy Dodge Cummings is the author of more than 25 books on topics ranging from hip-hop to Hillary Clinton. She came of age after the Beatles had already split up. However, Judy's three older brothers had a collection of Beatles albums that were the soundtrack of her childhood. As she researched this book, Judy created a playlist of Beatles songs to listen to and was happy to realize that she still knew the words to every song.